Mackenzie

by John Mackay

Lang**Syne**

PUBLISHING

WRITING *to* REMEMBER

Lang**Syne**

PUBLISHING

WRITING *to* REMEMBER

79 Main Street, Newtongrange,
Midlothian EH22 4NA
Tel: 0131 344 0414   Fax: 0845 075 6085
E-mail: info@lang-syne.co.uk
www.langsyneshop.co.uk

Design by Dorothy Meikle
Printed by Printwell Ltd
© Lang Syne Publishers Ltd 2016

ISBN 978-1-85217-060-8

Mackenzie

SEPT NAMES INCLUDE:

Charleson
Kenneth
Kennethson
MacBeolian
MacConnach
MacKerlich
MacVanish
MacVinish
Murchie
Murchieson

Mackenzie

MOTTO:
I shine, not burn.

CREST:
A Mountain Enflamed Proper.

PLANT BADGE:
Holly.

TERRITORY:
Kintail and at one time from Applecross right
across Scotland to the Moray Firth, covering
most of the old county of Ross and Cromarty
and including Strathconan and Strathgarve
(west of Dingwall), Strathpeffer and Beauly,
part of the Black Isle and part of Lewis in the
Outer Hebrides.

Chapter one:

The origins of the clan system

by Rennie McOwan

The original Scottish clans of the Highlands and the great families of the Lowlands and Borders were gatherings of families, relatives, allies and neighbours for mutual protection against rivals or invaders.

Scotland experienced invasion from the Vikings, the Romans and English armies from the south. The Norman invasion of what is now England also had an influence on land-holding in Scotland. Some of these invaders stayed on and in time became 'Scottish'.

The word clan derives from the Gaelic language term 'clann', meaning children, and it was first used many centuries ago as communities were formed around tribal lands in glens and mountain fastnesses.

The format of clans changed over the centuries, but at its best the chief and his family held the land on behalf of all, like trustees, and the ordinary clansmen and women believed they had a blood relationship with the founder of their clan.

There were two way duties and obligations. An inadequate chief could be deposed and replaced by someone of greater ability.

Clan people had an immense pride in race. Their relationship with the chief was like adult children to a father and they had a real dignity.

The concept of clanship is very old and a more feudal notion of authority gradually crept in.

Pictland, for instance, was divided into seven principalities ruled by feudal leaders who were the strongest and most charismatic leaders of their particular groups.

By the sixth century the 'British' kingdoms of Strathclyde, Lothian and Celtic Dalriada (Argyll) had emerged and Scotland, as one nation, began to take shape in the time of King Kenneth MacAlpin.

Some chiefs claimed descent from

ancient kings which may not have been accurate in every case.

By the twelfth and thirteenth centuries the clans and families were more strongly brought under the central control of Scottish monarchs.

Lands were awarded and administered more and more under royal favour, yet the power of the area clan chiefs was still very great.

The long wars to ensure Scotland's independence against the expansionist ideas of English monarchs extended the influence of some clans and reduced the lands of others.

Those who supported Scotland's greatest king, Robert the Bruce, were awarded the territories of the families who had opposed his claim to the Scottish throne.

In the Scottish Borders country – the notorious Debatable Lands – the great families built up a ferocious reputation for providing warlike men accustomed to raiding into England and occasionally fighting one another.

Chiefs had the power to dispense justice and to confiscate lands and clan warfare produced a society where martial virtues – courage, hardiness, tenacity – were greatly admired.

Gradually the relationship between the clans and the Crown became strained as Scottish monarchs became more orientated to life in the Lowlands and, on occasion, towards England.

The Highland clans spoke a different language, Gaelic, whereas the language of Lowland Scotland and the court was Scots and in more modern times, English.

Highlanders dressed differently, had different customs, and their wild mountain land sometimes seemed almost foreign to people living in the Lowlands.

It must be emphasised that Gaelic culture was very rich and story-telling, poetry, piping, the clarsach (harp) and other music all flourished and were greatly respected.

Highland culture was different from other parts of Scotland but it was not inferior or less sophisticated.

Central Government, whether in London or Edinburgh, sometimes saw the Gaelic clans as

*"The spirit of the clan means much
to thousands of people"*

a challenge to their authority and some sent expeditions into the Highlands and west to crush the power of the Lords of the Isles.

Nevertheless, when the eighteenth century Jacobite Risings came along the cause of the Stuarts was mainly supported by Highland clans.

The word Jacobite comes from the Latin for James – Jacobus. The Jacobites wanted to restore the exiled Stuarts to the throne of Britain.

The monarchies of Scotland and England became one in 1603 when King James VI of Scotland (1st of England) gained the English throne after Queen Elizabeth died.

The Union of Parliaments of Scotland and England, the Treaty of Union, took place in 1707.

Some Highland clans, of course, and Lowland families opposed the Jacobites and supported the incoming Hanoverians.

After the Jacobite cause finally went down at Culloden in 1746 a kind of ethnic cleansing took place. The power of the chiefs was curtailed. Tartan and the pipes were banned in law.

Many emigrated, some because they

wanted to, some because they were evicted by force. In addition, many Highlanders left for the cities of the south to seek work.

Many of the clan lands became home to sheep and deer shooting estates.

But the warlike traditions of the clans and the great Lowland and Border families lived on, with their descendants fighting bravely for freedom in two world wars.

Remember the men from whence you came, says the Gaelic proverb, and to that could be added the role of many heroic women.

The spirit of the clan, of having roots, whether Highland or Lowland, means much to thousands of people.

Chapter two:

Sons of Kenneth

The true origins of the Clan Mackenzie are not easy to find. It seems probable, however, that they sprang from an ancient Celtic family native to Scotland which had, well before the 12th century, controlled Wester Ross.

The Mackenzies of Kintail had possession of the great castle of Eilean Donan at the entrance to Loch Duich which for centuries was to be their chief stronghold. They held the land from the more senior branch of their family, the Earls of Ross, and when the Earldom passed into the hands of the Lord of the Isles the Mackenzies held Kintail for them.

Not until 1463 is there firm evidence of a direct grant of Kintail to the Mackenzies from the Crown.

The name Mackenzie means son of Kenneth, the Kenneth from whom they took their names having lived in the second half of the 13th century. He was the governor of Eilean Donan and lord of the other families who lived in Kintail under his sway. He was a powerful Lord and this fact appears to have strained his relationship with his relative William, Earl of Ross. This William was attempting to increase his influence over the Western Isles and so he wished to have greater personal control over such an important stronghold as Eilean Donan and Kenneth's presence there allowed William to try to take possession of the castle but Kenneth, supported by those people on the lands who looked to him as their lord, defended himself and refused to give up his home. Earl William, having been refused custody of the castle, sent a force of men to capture both it and Kenneth. There was a battle when Willaim's men assaulted the castle. Kenneth and his men defeated the attack and slaughtered the enemy. Another assault was planned but the Earl died before it could be carried out and his son who succeeded him became more involved with national affairs following the death of King Alexander III to bother about Eilean Donan.

This defeat of the Earl of Ross was important to Kenneth. It emphasised his personal standing as an independent chief with a notable following and it increased his power in the lands of Kintail. Kenneth died in 1304 and his son who succeeded him styled himself John McInnes and he was followed in this by succeeding generations who eventually adopted the style as a surname. As time went on, others in the land adopted the name too. Under the chief's protection and rule, they called themselves the children of Kenneth.

Chapter three:

Wars of Independence

**Kenneth's son John lived in the troubled times
of the Wars of Independence after Alexander
the Third died in 1286. There was a crisis in the
succession to the throne of Scotland and the
outcome was a war with England. In 1296
Edward the First, the Hammer of the Scots,
invaded Scotland and opposed the King John
Balliol, then established a government of
occupation but many of the Scots were not
prepared to submit to this form of regime and
war raged on for many years.**

Not until 1306 did Scotland find another
King. In that year Robert the Bruce had himself
crowned King at Scone and rebelled against the
English administration. But by no means all of the
Scots supported him in the course of the compli-
cated political struggle which preceded his coro-
nation. Bruce had killed his great rival, John the
Red Comyn, and so started a blood feud between

their two families. The Comyns, an immensely powerful family, would not support Bruce's bid for the throne and so he had to fight them as well as the English before he came to power. At first he fared badly. He was defeated almost immediately after his coronation at the battle of Methven and had to flee for safety to the Western Isles where he lay in hiding for some months. The two major powers in that part of Scotland were the Earl of Ross and Alexander of Argyll and both of them supported the Comyn side. The Earl of Ross was John Mackenzie's superior and Alexander of Argyll was his father-in-law but despite the pressure of these two influential men Mackenzie took the other side and, when Bruce sought shelter in early 1307, he was given it at Eilean Donan Castle. In later battles the Mackenzies fiercely

took the part of Bruce in spite of the dangerous opposition of their powerful neighbours. Mackenzie, of course, was rewarded for his support and when Bruce won his cause the clan began to enjoy more favour and prosperity.

First they were able to assert even more strongly their independence from the greater families such as the Earls of Ross to whom they had been subject. This caused much jealousy and rivalry which took the form of long, lasting and bitter feuds, particularly with the MacDonald Lord of the Isles. Later in the wars, Bruce found more support in the West Highlands and the Isles and at the Battle of Bannockburn, that great clash which finally secured Scotland's freedom, several thousand of Bruce's men from the West were led by Mackenzie from Kintail. His support for Bruce was the first

example of service to the Scottish Crown over many generations and was to make his family influential in the north, although at times unpopular.

The struggle for power and status was not over, though. In the time of John's successor, Kenneth of the Noose, the Earls of Ross took advantage of some weaknesses of the Mackenzies and try to reassert their old authority. The Highlands at this time were particularly lawless and raiding and feuding proved stronger than the law. On one occasion the Earl's men raided Mackenzie land at Kinlochewe and while they carried off their booty Mackenzie and his men gave chase. They captured much of the loot and killed a good number of the raiders. This of course displeased the Earl of Ross who had Kenneth captured and later executed at Inverness. The lands of Kintail were given over to a supporter of Ross's who failed, however, to capture Eilean Donan or Kenneth's son, Murdoch Dhu who was only a child when his father died. He turned the Earls out of his land and claimed his heritage and for the rest of his time concentrated on rebuilding his family's position.

Chapter four:

The blood is strong

In 1362 David the Second confirmed Murdoch in his rights to Kintail and Eilean Donan. Murdoch's son who succeeded him in 1375 was apparently responsible for a particularly evil deed. He was known as Murdoch of the Bridge and an old manuscript tells how he earned the nickname.

After his marriage he and his wife lived together for some years without any children. Being born for a Highland chieftainship, in those days childlessness verged on disgrace and it certainly would be a slight on his manhood and so, thinking more of his manhood than his wife, he resolved to be rid of her so that he would be free to marry again. He thus arranged that she should be thrown over the Bridge of Scattel into the turbulent waters of the River Conon to her death but she survived the fall and as it turned out she was carrying a child which also survived.

Murdoch, of course, was penitent as soon as heard this news and lived happily with her and his son for the rest of his life

At the end of the 14th century the MacDonald Lords of the Isles obtained the Earldom of Ross. They were by this time immensely powerful and were almost independent rulers in the west. The Mackenzies were, of course, normally under their sway. The Lords of the Isles in trying to maintain and increase their power naturally came into conflict with the royal authorities and for much of the 15th century the story of many of the clans is concerned very closely with the fluctuating struggles which ended with loss of the Isles to the Crown in 1411.

Donald, Lord of the Isles, decided to try to take actual possession of the landlord parts of the Earldom of Ross. He gathered a great army of clansmen and marched right across Scotland heading for Aberdeen. There was great fear in the country but he was stopped before reaching his goal at Harlaw. A famous battle was fought there which has lived ever since in Scottish folklore and, although neither side won a convincing victory, Donald had to return home to the isles. Mackenzie was one of the chiefs who had refused to lead out his clan in support of his superior on this occasion. He repeatedly refused to support the Lord of the Isles so in the end came off worse a few years after Harlaw. The Lord had to submit to Crown superiority several times. Throughout the 15th century there were rebellions against the Crown as a result of which much of the Lordship's land was forfeited and eventually even the title Lord of the Isles was surrendered to the Crown. The Mackenzies had consistently refused to support their normal Lords who, of course, lost no opportunity to wreak vengeance upon them for the part they had played in the weakening of their power. The old feud between the Mackenzies and the MacDonalds raged ever stronger. Shortly before the forfeiture of the Lordship, an attempt was made to heal the breach by Marion, the Mackenzie heir to the daughter of the Lord of the Isles. The plan looked hopeful and a nephew of the Lord of the Isles living near the Mackenzie lands at Balconie invited

Mackenzie to a great Christmas feast but there was
no room in the house for all the guests and
Mackenzie was asked to sleep the night in an out-
house. This he took as a great affront and fighting
almost broke out there and then but Mackenzie
hastily left and returned to Strathpeffer which by
then had become the main seat of the Mackenzie
chief where his father the old chief lived. From
there, still enraged about the insult, he sent his
wife, a MacDonald, back to her clan, determined
to have none of that name in his house. In a particularly cruel gesture, taking advantage of the fact
that she was blind in one eye, he sent her to
MacDonald on a one-eyed horse accompanied by
a one-eyed servant with a one-eyed dog following
behind her. It is aid that the grief which this
episode caused was responsible for her death.

      Trouble was now inevitable. Mackenzie
immediately went to Lord Lovat's house where he
demanded Lovat's daughter for a wife and Lovat,
bowing to the force, assented and so Mackenzie
thus married bigamously, adding yet another
insult to the MacDonald estate. The outcome was

a battle. MacDonald sent to the Isles for men and an army of 3000 was raised which came across Scotland, attacked Inverness, plundered much of the north east and then marched back through Strathconnon, ravaging the Mackenzie land and putting to the sword many of the people they found there. They arrived at last at a church which they set on fire although terrified old men, women and children had taken shelter and so burned them all to death.

This massacre was the final straw for Mackenzie.

On the following day, despite the fact that he had fewer warriors, he met the MacDonalds in a battle known as the Battle of the Parks. The Mackenzies, only about 600 in number, attacked first and immediately retreated again so drawing the MacDonalds after them into a marshy piece of land where they could not easily move As soon as they were more or less trapped, a hidden body of Mackenzie archers attacked them and killed many. Then the rest of the Mackenzies attacked again. There was fierce fighting with the chiefs undertaking single combat and many men were killed. There are countless stories of individual and bloodthirsty acts of heroism in the fight but in the end the MacDonalds got the worst of it. Those who remained alive fled for their lives.

This was only one incident amongst many in the feud but this battle had national consequences since it greatly weakened the MacDonald power, the Mackenzies benefiting by supporting the Crown against its opponents thus taking in more favour and with that favour came land and influence.

The final forfeiture of the Lordship of the Isles in 1493 removed the most formidable opponent to Mackenzie advancement and through the 16th century the Mackenzies were to be so favoured by the Crown that their fortunes and influence were almost unrivaled. Their power could be used for or against the Crown but it could also be used purely for their own advancement. Like most clans in those days the Mackenzies were not beyond using their power over weaker clans by fair means or foul to increase their own possessions. A notable example of this is placed towards the end of the 16th century when the MacLeods of Lewis were very weak, having been torn apart by internal dissension. Mackenzie of Kintail became involved in this struggle through family connections. He came down on one side of the dispute and lent his power to that branch of the Lewis family. There was much fighting in which Mackenzie was deeply embroiled. These disturbances on Lewis came to the attention of King James the Sixth whose government was determined to end them and at the same time be in profit from civilising the land. The MacLeods were forfeited and their lands given to a group of lowland gentry known as the Fife Adventurers. They were to colonise the island and make profitable its fishing industry.

Publicly Mackenzie supported this move but in secret he did nothing to help it. The Adventurers failed to overcome the stout resistance of the Lewis men and also failed to take possession of the island. The experiment was tried again and again. Mackenzie appeared to help but in secret worked against the interests of the government. When the Adventurers went home for a second time Mackenzie stepped in, using his family links with the MacLeods, his favour in government circles and his power in the north. He bought the rights to Lewis from the Fifers, received the King's approval of the purchase and actually occupied the land. He persecuted the family of the MacLeod chief until there was none left to oppose him and thus added Lewis to the territories of the Mackenzies.

Chapter five:

Family fortunes

In the 17th century the Mackenzies reached the peak of their fortune. In 1609 the chief was given the title Lord Mackenzie of Kintail and in 1623 the greatest honour of all was given to him – the Earldom of Seaforth. By this time the Mackenzies had moved their main seat to Brahan near Dingwall where they built a fine castle.

But James, the Earl of Seaforth, had to flee to France in the Revolution of 1689 because of his support of the Stuarts. When the Old Pretender returned to try and reclaim his throne, Seaforth came to his help but to no avail. He was forced to surrender to Mackay, the government general, and was imprisoned until 1697. He then left the country for France and joined his exiled King. When he died, the family's fortunes were beginning to suffer. Warfare and absence of their chief and the disfavour of the government all took their toll on the productivity of the land and the financial state of the family but worse was to come.

William the Fifth Earl lived in France until 1713 when he returned to Scotland. Only two years later was he deeply involved in the plotting which started the 1715 Jacobite Rebellion. He was one of the chiefs who met at Aboyne supposedly for a hunt but with the real intention of planning a rebellion. When the Rising actually started, Seaforth led about 3000 men southward to join the main Jacobite army. The Rebellion failed. The only major battle that was fought was at Sheriffmuir near Stirling. It did not last long and who had won was unclear. Each army had been defeated on one wing and victorious on the other. They each claimed victory but in any case the Rebellion was over. There had been heavy casualties in the battle of which the Mackenzies had their full share. There are lists of those killed and the name Mackenzie occurs as often as any other. The army soon melted away as the clansmen, disheartened, went home.

In February, 1716, King James went back to France with Seaforth amongst those who accompanied him. The Earl was branded a traitor and the estates were once again forfeited. In practice, though, the government found it impossible to take control of the Mackenzie lands. Several attempts to force the people to pay to the government factors were met with stout resistance. The clan recognised no superiors but their chief and would pay no other man what they owed to him.

In 1718 another attempt was made to put James back on the throne. A large Spanish fleet was despatched for Scotland but a great storm scattered it long before it reached the Scottish coast. Only two of the ships arrived but one of them carried Seaforth who landed at Eilean Donan and raised his clansmen at Kintail. However, again they did not get far. They were defeated in a skirmish at Glenshiel and Seaforth, badly wounded, once again had to fly to the Continent with a price on his head. As a result of this totally unsuccessful rising the government's commander in the north ordered that Eilean Donan, for so many centuries a stronghold of the Mackenzies, should be blown up and demolished. The romantic castle, of which we see so many photographs today, was restored by a Mackenzie during the last century from the ruins of the old building.

In 1741 the estates were sold back to the Seaforth family, the government having totally failed to gain any control over them. But by this time the lands had been so ravaged by warfare that they were poor and unprofitable. The Earl's fortune was meagre and he now lacked the influence and power of his predecessors. The Fifth Earl, who had been pardoned and who returned to Scotland in 1726 died in 1740 but because the title was still formally forfeit his son and successor Kenneth was known as Lord Fortrose. He was rarely in the Highlands and did not support the 1745 uprising. But the clan system was destined for extinction although their famous fighting spirit was required for the American War of Independence and other colonial activities in 1778 when the famous regiment, the Seaforth Highlanders, was raised from Mackenzie clansmen.

Eilean Donan Castle